Mercy Is a Bright Darkness

Mercy Is a Bright Darkness

Selected Poems on Our Connectedness to Each Other through Nature's Elements and Seasons

Lisa Fosmo

2023

GOLDEN DRAGONFLY PRESS

AMHERST, MASSACHUSETTS

FIRST PRINT EDITION, September 2023
FIRST EBOOK EDITION, October 2023

ISBN: 979–8–9882025–8–5

Library of Congress Control Number: Requested

Printed on acid-free paper supplied by a Forest Stewardship Council-certified provider. First published in the United States of America by Golden Dragonfly Press, 2023.

www.goldendragonflypress.com

To my incredible husband, Craig
for his continued encouragement, love, and support.
I love you.

To Clark, Meredith, and Sophia, who are a constant source of pride.
You are so loved.

With admiration and love to my parents.

Contents

Spring on Lake Michigan

I would like to say to you,
dear bringer of new,
the one holding a pinecone
in the cold early newness of spring.
There bundled in awkwardness
from the corner of the earth's room.

Though I never told you,
you are my favorite season.
My favorite smell as I breathe in
the birth of new, listen to birds arriving,
shooting like stars across the night sky
on a feathered whim.

The ice seems to be riding a floor jack,
rising till it will break.
There must be a crack somewhere,
where the river's thaw has entered
spilling beneath the crust like a secret.
Waiting to break out onto hurried waters,
but I can see no breaks.

Only in the night I hear the war
of winter losing its battle to spring.
The sound like gunfire.
The loud thunder of ice popping.

And I'm taking sides.
I'm rooting for spring.
Praying this new ruler won't turn.
Praying she won't spill water in her hurry.

Praying she heeds her time knowing,
no one has loved her better or more.
Until winter comes again, with all the
elegance of a new bride and we will
love her all the more all over again.

Today I wait for that moment.
Where once again; I will hear the roar
of rushing waters into the thaw of waves
crashing. The very sound that rattles
Heaven's door.

Even the Turn of Winter

How a thin sheet holds our heat
enough to survive,
the calamity of an old furnace.
How the steam of wolf hunger
rises in the woods.
The copper burn of beard grass
from the snow.
How the sheath of ice on
plum blossoms holds safety.
The
wooden bowl of
blood oranges
Stain
our fingers and tongues
with hope.
Outside
the Forsythia with all its
might, blooms
its yellow fury at the
dark smoke of a
tobacco sky.
Even the turn of winter,
its slow fade
holds us,
as we turn towards warmth.

I can wait for spring

For I know where beauty sleeps

dreaming a secret

Hummingbird Water

Spring is carried by
the return of nesting birds,
both big and small.

And what is a hummingbird,
but air mixed with nirvana
Lite by a spark, a spit of fire.

To know spring is to know forgiveness
and the return of things gone
Like the spring carnival
That comes too soon.
The air too cool.

The steel gate entrance to a ride
Its cold steel trap door
slams shut then springs open
to things that flutter and green.

There the spinning of color and warm light .
The smell of spun sugar electric alive.
Marvel at its warm cotton candy wonder
A slice of clown hair served on a cardboard stick.

It melts the words on my tongue
I want to melt it with rain.
Make hummingbird water.

I long for spring
I need to say it out loud.
Walk with the words in my pocket.

Sprinkle them where things don't grow.
Feed them to hungry geese and swans
and offer them to crows and sparrows.

Sugar up all the bees.
Awaken
the bumblebee queen
waiting alone in her winter cave.

An elixir,
a love potion
to welcome hummingbirds.
The air still cold
It begins to sprinkle.
If only I could melt
live as nectar.

Become hummingbird water.
All the while spinning,
spinning like sugar,
on the spring carnival tilt-a whirl.

At the St. Vincent DePaul Thrift Store

I can feel Easter on my skin
as the sun comes in.
A plate in my hand,
at the ST. Vincent DePaul thrift store.

These dishes are just like the ones
my grandmother had.
The little blue flowers peek out
from the milk white snow of bone China.
These are the dishes of my childhood Easter.

Carrots round as pennies,
sliced jewels,
the color of tangerine
and persimmon, that
shine in saffron butter.

Tender roast beef
the kind a knife isn't required
and crispy chicken,
creamy mashed potatoes
dressed in velvet gravy,

sweet ambrosias,
hot dinner rolls,
and let's not forget
the Easter cake
Saved
best for last.

Jellybeans and
Sayklly's fudge eggs,
"Happy Easter" pipped
in bold yellow frosting.
This day holds no rules,
candy is for breakfast.

Spring, oh how my grandmother loved it,
how crocus, then tulips, and daffodils
rise from the earth towards heaven,
like a green Jesus ascending.

Hearing the hymns sung on Easter Sunday
in chorus with returning birds.
Yes, I can feel Easter,

I can feel spring even in winter,
even at the ST. Vincent De Paul thrift store.
I can feel it like the anticipation of the cake
still in the kitchen.

A Bear's Elegy / Looking for You

A tribute to Judith Minty

Wind breaths through trees differently here and whispers on breath,
yellow dog, gray wolf, black bear. When I last saw the bear outside
    my cabin,
I heard the loud clash of cymbals crashing, as the bear ran for her life
    with two cubs trailing
free… She was only looking for you.

The fires I kindle and tend to, the fiery breath the wood stove spits
    back from
the small log sauna house as I bathe with buckets and scoops. In the
    night air
I watch the steam escape my flesh like secret lives my bones betray as
    I stand
naked beneath your stars.

When I last saw the bear, he stood on haunches of back legs and
    peered into
my car, with eyes of copper kettles that filled with honeycombs, as I
    tried to leave.
He was only looking for you.

How cold bites at me or the heat of a summer night is forgotten on
    the sound of wolves Howling.
I hear them barking at me like territorial dogs from the rocky ledge.
    As you know nights are
filled with wolves and bears.

When I last saw the bear, his massive paw prints haunt me as I
    often saw them
pressed into mud and sacred loam. He was only looking for you.

Hidden in minerals mined from the earth, no more precious than
    breath riding the breeze on
blueberry scent, that fuels the forests lungs, on thick black fur.

When I last saw the bear he was pounding, pounding his great paws
    into rock moaning
thundering with all his weight. As if to say do not linger in my
    discomfort!
We said nothing to the bear, my dog and I. He was only looking
    for you.

Dancing the darkness at its dreams. To its very edge, and still I do
    not know how to speak
or even whisper in bear voice.

I know we have both touched waters that have washed over the same
    rocks.
I have learned that fear belongs to the bear. And when a bear dies he
is
    just the snow
that melts away, folded into riverbanks of waters that wash over our
    same rocks.

When I last saw the bear, he lives on in legends and poems and in|
    your dreams...

We were only looking for you.

A Serving of Peace

Early January walk,
sky's fevered white dream
covers all in stillness.

In a world suspended
perfect and new.
Nothing seems fragile.
Yet I search for a small wound.

An evergreen branch given way,
broken by the heavy burden
of such beauty.

A branch chickadees
and blue jays graced
only hours before.

Build the altar,
cover the table in white cloth.
A large platter made of milk glass,
add some fallen treasure,
the fragrant pine branch,
a pinecone, a few feathers.

A candle, light pulses
through its glass sheath.

A few coveted smooth stones
from summer's path.

Birds of white porcelain,
others iron and shadow.
A bundle of white sage.

And this peace,
this embrace, embodies
the celebration kindling
beneath the snow.

For it could never
be enough to
just survive winter.

To My Babies with Love

Time seasons the bloom,
awakens the goddess
to plumes formed in secret waters.

I know it in the still hush of night.
The sweet baby bathing in the milk of the moon.

How the sunrise comes soft and pink
a lullaby to the night.

When both my babies live this side of my flesh.
I count days they are mine
before the world owns them 280 to be exact
if there is any exactness to be had.

The days tip and the moon counts out more,
and I have less of these.
Time alone to comfort and nurse them
while the world sleeps.

To hold little fingers and little toes.
In their eyes stars and constellations
a universe yet untold.

Together we are awake in love.
In this new life the world unfolds
a discovery of all god can touch.

A Love on Fire

My dear child,
I will protect you with all that I am.
As I carry a fierce fire around me.

Because it is at the center
that I hold you near.
You are rooted there
how fire breaks open seeds.
It was then that I grew you
in my heart.

I set you free in the world
to your own beautiful fire.
Always remember this warmth,
long after I've gone and turned to ash.

Know you are never lost to me.
For I will be the sage burning,
just follow the shadow of my smoke.

The Edge of Foxfire

A great fire quickened outside our window,
a fox rushed near our door, and across our land
it didn't stop, only ran past. So fast as not to touch us.
Not to take a thing, only brushed by.

In folklore and some native cultures,
It is said the Fox can warn of impending death.
Others believe they are healers of the sick.
Some believe they are Gods of the sun,
and bring blessings of wisdom and joy.

When my daughter was small,
She feared the Fox's Erie screams,
Sweet girl, it is only a fox singing a blessing,
calling the sunrise.

Our daughter has fallen gravely ill,
Her body wracked with pain and illness.
Lines and tubes, shots of anticoagulants,
light her belly, like bio Luminescent blue
green suns. Foxfire in full bloom.

Grateful to the fox that ran swiftly that night,
and didn't stop to touch us or take a thing.
Not that night, not now, not yet.
Only blazed past. Brushed us with a blessing

How many times we dissolve into night,
so many deaths before we die.
Each rise and fall into darkness.

Seeking to evoke the sun again, a calling out,
how my great-grandmother had, making medicines
from plants and herbs.

I want to pronounce them in prayer,
these mortal earthly names for the sun.
Saffron, Yarrow, Tansy, Poppy, Echinacea, Marigold,
Dandelion, Feverfew, Ginseng, Goldenseal, Chamomile.
My prayer, my offering standing in the glow of Foxfire.

Still, I want to pretend each time that it's early
and no one is leaving, no one has died.
I want to believe we are not just ghosts
waiting to shed our skin.
I want the fox,
over and over
Blessings us at dawn.

Small Islands

We have lost and won wars
of our own. We are broken,
but still here.

The war has just begun in Ukraine.
Helpless, I purchase a quilt.
White with stitched doves.

Place it over the once bed
of my daughter's childhood.
A white flag of peace.

She lives through days prior
that seemed impossible.
This is my Surrender

The world like most things
is bigger than all of us.
Still I build an altar each year.

All white with birds, sage,
an occasional green bow.
A serving of peace.

It's become clear the need
for Small islands
to visit in times like these.

A Fox in Drought Season

Any day of a dry season
sedge and wood are
crisp shadows for tinder

In the morning we can see
smoke across the lake.
The Hiawatha forest is burning.

Friends evacuate,
move their horses to safety.
In the distance the concussive clamor
of propane tanks exploding as they flee.

We post Smokey the Bear signs
with slogans;
"Only you can prevent forest fires"
and "Fires kill".

Who decided a bear wearing bib overalls
and a hat equals safety.
We do it anyway.

As if the words somehow make paper
safe from fire. As if paper was a cure
for carelessness or flames.

At the edge of the forest,
a blaze of fire,
a glorious bushy tail.

A mask of flames,
to golden eyes.
A chest of snow,
a puff of cloud.
A spirit.

The fox doesn't turn or run.
Are her kits hidden nearby?
Does she feel the air is ripe
for kindling?

This stillness,
a communion,
 waiting for the sky
to gather and Conjure.

We must believe in clouds.
That they can hold an ocean.
It only takes a small crack
For prayers to fall like rain.

Sparks on Ice

In early hours the
amorous screams
of fox, travel the ice,
and the hollow
of bare trees.
On a lazy Saturday,
winter's arctic temperatures
hold us captive.
We sip cups of warmth
from our back window.
The day's entertainment,
the ice on the bay.
It's mating season
for the fox. They greet
as nimble sparks on ice
bounce,
and bow
a courtship
do si do.
Prance
the fox trot,
the rumba,
the electric slide
on lightning legs.
Their silly antics
and exuberant joy.
Soon …
the kits of spring.

Seven Reasons to Call Your Mother

One. So she can tell me about the scarlet tanager outside her window.

Two. To say I love you, as she never tires of hearing it.

Three. To hear her voice, try to memorize the rise and hum.

Four. To ask her for prayers, because no one will ever pray for you the way a mother prays for her child.

Five. To tell her my daughter survived another night in the ICU.

Six. Because time runs shorter than we can ever know.

Seven. The Scarlet Tanager is now outside my window.

Indigo Bunting

The birds from my 20's and 30's
were lovely and magical.
There were and still are robins and blue jays,
starlings and grackles, among others,
but Indigo buntings seemed so exotic!

Traded now for Scarlet Tanagers.
Where have the buntings all gone?
And when did the tanagers come?

As I sit and listen for bird voices.
In my mind I travel back.
where there is no sound, as
I scrape the bowl with a silicone-coated spoon.
My tiny daughter's open baby bird mouth
to mushy white cereal. I take her outside
show her off to the indigo bunting at our feeder.

I want to pretend we too are colorful birds.
My little sparrow and I.
I want her to love all the birds.
Their bodies of song and air

In the hope she may have Indigo buntings
of her own someday, among doves and starlings,
grackles, and robins, blue jays and chickadees,
with scarlet tanagers
to flame the trees when she least expects it.

Bathing Beauties

Inside the quest bedroom at my brother's house,
my mother lies, nestled between my sister and I
in her plush pink robe, my sister in blue satin
and me in cotton navy stripes.

Mom winces, pointing her toes like a ballerina,
as her leg tightens into a charlie horse.
she kicks her leg and stretches.

We begin in solidarity throwing our legs up
in unison, higher and higher. Our arms carve air,
turning our heads in sync, as if they were adorned
in flowered rubber caps.

We are Esther Williams bathing beauties, we are
synchronized swimming, laughing unexpectedly,
with our whole bodies. Throwing our heads back
trying to catch our breath on foamy linen waves.

My father hasn't been gone a day yet.
Already we have traveled so far in the moment.
We expect grief to shatter us, to break us open,
but no one tells you about the fluidity of joy.

How it sneaks in, seeps into every crack
and fissure like a salve. Soaks you to your core
poured from some unknown vessel of mercy.

No one warns you there will be joy.
And in that fresh jubilant, flowing glee,
I want to whisper to my father
we haven't forgotten you.
We've only gone for a swim

The Rain between Seasons /
Mothers and Daughters

The waves broke beyond my smallness,
and I was toppled. My lips purple,
tiny violets shivering, at only four years old.

And yet, I wouldn't stop until she came for me.
Her colorful beach towel open arms
a rainbow sopping me up like a stray drop.

The smell of pine in the air as a storm brewed.
I see now how the breath of rain sits between us.
How one good rain is often all that rests
between the seasons.
How a wave can topple you.
How one storm could take you.

How I'm told women of a certain age
all seem to have the same mother.
How one woman's mother slipped
on the ice and she couldn't recover.

How another woman's mother is so forgetful now,
and she hides her keys to keep her safe.
How someday it might not be dents that result,
but something she can't take back.

How another woman's mother often forgets to eat now.
So she brings her dinner and sits with her.
Her mother gets angry says she isn't hungry
before her own hunger forgets her words.

I do all I can to listen and understand,
as I do not yet have this mother.
Suddenly, I find myself grateful, for the conversation
with my own mother, who made the wise decision
to give up her car, Asking if today I could please pick
up the books she ordered from the library.

But only of course if the storm doesn't come.
Now I can see how the breath of rain sits between us all.
How one good rain is often
all that rests between the seasons.

How a wave can topple you
How the tide can hide you even from yourself,
how one storm can take you.
And how it's my turn now to wade out
arms wide open holding all the colors.

Bodies of Water

Swim, dream, and come up for air.

All night long I dream of swimming
naked with my husband on the shores of Nahma
The moon sees our perfect young bodies.

I remember how years later we taught our kids
to swim racing waves in suits of Blue,
red and pink nylon skins.

Bathing our baby son in the kitchen sink.
His delight chewing on the washcloth,
a wooden spoon in his other small hand
a tiny rubber duck bobs at his chubby little toes.

The warm basin draped across our bed on towels
and sheets on a cold November morning as I bathe
our newborn daughter. Her delicate arms and legs
flail in a warm, watery memory of her life days prior.

Morning gales speak to me
of mid-August leaning hard into autumn.
The sound of waves lulls me to sleep
and wakes me before the light.

Floating in on a ghostly billow of sheer white curtains
this same sound accompanies me on my morning walk.
Outside, the damp air hits my eyes washes them
as if I've just been swimming.

The wind whirls my hair like a wild mane
of a mermaid in a squall. Passing by familiar trees
they too shimmer and swirl their own synchronized swim
on last full green leaves.

A dance to end summer and awaken fall.
I carry these all with me, how the moon holds
the memory of water moving.

We entangle in the impossible of yesterday and today
like an elbow sticking out of nowhere in the waves.
I dive in to memories, reach down to the sacrum
and kiss the rippled spine of it all.

Summer waves call out

Trade candy toes and tan lines

Come be a mermaid

The Spirit of Water

We are all hunters of water.
Haunted since our first swim,
that dive into our mother's pool,
the dark trenches of her body.

We draw from her spring
the lake of our breath.
From our lives
salted little oceans fall.

You will know them all
by name, by the continents
they reside. Trace each
thread, each vein back to
the great spirit.

The empathy of water is known
to us all on the oxen tongues of
harvest and prairie bees, here to sip
beads of mercy in morning dew.

We are all bound by water.
The great spirit of water is here,
how it always is. We carry it with us,
in the container of our bodies.

The Voice of Water

All water is related,
one family,
one entity.
A shapeshifter,
traveling,
speaking
on a cloud,
a shower,
a rainbow,
a feather of snow.

Stand near
the highway,
close your eyes
to hear the ocean.

 Stand near
Lake Michigan
and hear
the highway
talk over her.

Sit with the ice
on the frozen bay,
Just to hear it sing.

Go to the rushing river,
listen; you will hear it,
hum like a swarm
calling it all back
to the hive.

The End of an Era

We didn't know enough
to hold on to it.
The harness of wild.
The lake a love,
a wild beast.

These steel whales
the workhorses,
the last of the great ships,
become ghosts of our
memories and dreams.
Over one hundred and fifty
years of history,
on Little Bay de Noc.

Deep into the night
a familiar sound.
The unmistakable
rhythmic hum
of the engine.
The thump of waves
echoes a melodic call.
A large ore ship
cuts her way through
the channel.

Take notice,
all too aware this may be
the last.

What an honor to be awake
to steal this moment with her.
All dressed in her glory.
What a beauty she is
dazzled in layers of light,
appearing as if jewels of some lady
of great wealth and refinement.

What a gift to get a glance
at this treasure, a comfort,
a part of home and life
on the Great Lakes.

The shipping of ore
into our port
has ended.

A whale song
no longer
carried to us,
across
the backbone
of Lake Michigan.

Bitten by the Moon

Fierce fallen moon
a fire opal
at two in the morning

Nests the horizon,
lingers, catches fire.

A deep orange embered flare
An egg-shaped sail
anchored on the bay.

The water all aglow
with the moon's
admiration of the sun.

The lake holds the moon
in its palm as it flickers,

a mirror to the sun.
Dreams itself into a hatchling
a Phoenix on rise.

As Lake Michigan gentles
tender where the fire's
teeth have touched.

Our Moon Song

Granddaughter,
do you remember
how we sang
to the moon.
That it was
made of butter.
A melt of time
a turn of tide
to fiery red days,
round ripe pearls.
This generational torch,
a legacy passed on
when my grandmother carried me
inside my mother.
How my mother carried my daughter
Inside of me
Each our own maiden's purse.
A loot of tiny pearls,
of many moons.
This ends where it began
in sacred red earth
where all our moons fall.
I carried my son's daughter too.
Yes, you granddaughter.
Not with my womb but my heart.

Remnants of Constellations

I want to sit
on the mountain
in the dark of night
all alone with the stars,

and the memory of ancestors
shining down,
and the wonder of those yet born.

In the smoke, fire and dust
That built us.
In the gears of the galaxies
own time machine.
To be that close to what lights us all.

My Grandfather Was an El Camino

He was child labor in a work camp.
He was the orange he stole
to save his dying sister.
My grandfather was tobacco,
he was beer and whiskey.
He was baked beans and ice cream.
My grandfather was puppies and dogs
and loyalty, he was sawdust, and pockets
of money. He was wide grins, and All-star wrestling.
My grandfather was a black velvet painting
of the last supper. He was rows of church pews,
he built after his church burned.
My grandfather was all the letters of the alphabet
when my grandmother taught him to read and write.
He was heart attacks, and diabetes, He was bread
and butter, red meat and venison stew.
He was the box of crackerjacks with the prize.
He was nicknames and french slang.
My grandfather was Christmas trees sold in the city.
He was stick built homes in our town,
He was rooftops and banks, kitchens and cabinets.
He was carved wooden dolls dancing.
He was a boy without a childhood.
My grandfather was a father to daughters
and a son born sleeping.
He was fresh water for horses,
and dry blankets when they were cold and wet.
My grandfather was a plane and a bird flying over.
He was garlands and Christmas lights
strung across Ludington Street.
He was all golden with a pinstripe,

He was the path and line running
through our lives and veins
My grandfather was an El Camino

The Arrival

My brother's early morning call
to say dad's next to me on the front seat...

It's just the two of you
Father and son, one last time.
He doesn't expect you to be so warm.
Your ashes not yet cool, as
you travel back to us.

I think Rumi said it best
"you broke the cage and flew"

At what point do we really leave?
Does anyone know with certainty
when the soul leaves the body?
How far, or how long it lingers,
where do we wonder?
In this mystery,
this infinite continuum.

Today I want to believe it's you,
that drives up to my house
I catch myself,
as the van moves on,
it is not you.

Your body now annulled from your life,
but you already arrive
on a red bird, a cardinal
for my sister.

Then become a blue jay
a scarlet tanager. A song
through the car radio.
Led Zeppelin, "All of My Love"

Some things will remain, and live on
in this mystery, and never really leave,
how love never ends…

Ruby Slippers

The Golf Masters is on today.
As you sleep in these weeks,
the sun shines
the world greens.
A robin sings at your window,
yet all your ramparts repeal
crumble to dust.

It's strangely cold
In that corner hospice room,
where we watch old
black and whites,
Johnny Weissmüller as Tarzan.

Watch the vivid color of
The Wizard of Oz.
Years ago we visited The Smithsonian
and Dorothy's Ruby slippers.
You took me to see Bambi and Dumbo,
how I cry each time
at the lesson of loss.

I step outside to make a call.
An old woman in a wheelchair calls out…
Wait, please take me with you.
She appears like an old movie star, or a Disney Queen,
in her bright red lipstick and colorful turban wrapped head.
She smiles, her long knobby fingers reach out
as if for an apple, or to grasp her wish to go home.

Aren't we all on our way home every day inching closer.
If only I could grant her wish, and Dorothy's Ruby slippers.
Instead, I offer a bit of my heart. The nurse wheels her away,
we wave and she blows a kiss.

When I return you are still asleep. I hold your hand,
the Golf Masters is still on, and the announcer whispers
as if not to wake you,
not to interrupt your soft journey home.

The Laughter of Owls

Owls are legends
Peer into darkness,
a warning,
a protection,
a silent feathering.

A gather of Owls
is called a Parliament,
a blessing of wisdom.
A gift from the Goddess
Athena

A weekend at the cabin,
a packed bag
complete with classics,
and books written
by author friends.

The books sit idle on the side table.
Instead, I dream they are all here tonight,
Giggling like girls at summer camp.
Laughter is the vocabulary of night owls.

Awakened by the loud chatter of owl
voices as they cachenate over the lake.
The sound echoes of laughter,
preludes a sleepy saunter,
to the outhouse.

The smell of a freshly
smoked cigarette

trails near the outhouse,
lingers in the small room.

At first I think it is only
a poet friend
out for a last smoke.
Or maybe,
Mary Oliver chain smoking
In the woods.
Or maybe Anne Sexton ,
Smoking after a steamy confession,
Or Sylvia Plath smoking in secret
how she once had.
I'm too tired to be alarmed.
Yet no one's here to smoke.
The Owls are quiet now.
Loons sing lullabies
Time to dream of other things.

The mystery of dreams.
The laughter of Owls
The bonds of friendship

I wonder who dreamed
of being here?
Perhaps somewhere
a dear poet friend
is smoking a cigarette.
out under the stars.
The last of the night.

A reminder another day waits,
Where Hummingbirds sip at the feeder,
Cranes lurch on the shore.

Robin's red breast,
a midwifery of small blue worlds.
Owls call into nightfall

The poem inside the poem.
The books waiting to be read
The song longing for ears.
The cigarette burning miles away,
and tonight we are
Owls laughing in a dream.

A Yooper Takes Shelter at Camp

The sticky fingers of the forest,
pat my head, comb my hair
as I pass under pine branches.
A makeshift path through a mix
of winter and spring where there
is no driving in close.

I become pack mule,
a pachyderm carrying cargo,
a gypsy with sacks of food,
gallons of water, bottles of magic
and cans of craft beer.

My love busy building a fire,
priming the water pump, chopping ice
blocking the outhouse door.
The outdoor shower a heave of ice and leaves.

I empty my boots, free the gems of winter
that catch as my feet sink snow to hip.
My afternoon perch a stepladder
on the covered porch,
washing large windows
eyes to the lake still thick with ice.

The neighbor's dog runs over for a visit
suckles and mouthes my dangling barefoot
like a calf at an udder. She's an old friend
cries and whines not understanding this
new world, and why we hadn't stopped by.

I find forgiveness in her generous brown eyes
with my offering of chicken scrapes.

At dusk one lone crane flies by
feathers in close more shadow than bird.
We watch the fire from the glass door
of the wood stove, flaming orange and quick
as a litter of fox kits.
The radio tuned to 103.3 Elmer Aho
bringing us comfort with old country and folk music.
His soft, familiar Fozzy Bear voice
a Saturday evening Yooper Companion.

One last peek at an endless starry sky.
We nuzzle in bed. The dark so large
so peaceful it eats the world.
We came here to be small to disappear.
We drift off belonging now to the ever
widening quiet, waiting for the gift of morning.

A Moose Calf at Midnight

We awaken to the young
cries of an animal.
My husband whisperers
something is lost.
I whisper back,
or lost someone.

We peer out
from the cabin
at the vast blackness.
We know this cry,
It is a moose calf.

Years first bloom.
A wiry copper whorl.
A sapling in the
thick marshlands.
The woods dense of
balsam, birch and maple.

Oh little one
how new the dark
of your world.

Your mother,
brown mountain,
wooly coat of
bronzed brawn.
Where has she gone?

I am an old mother.
Something primal,
ingrained in my
marrows field,
aches…

Your lonely calls,
like a needle stabbing
the night. Powerless,
we are threaded
to its stitch of nothing.

We wait for peace.
A small fire warms us.
My head rests on the
flannel of his shoulder.
We are together in this
aloneness.

When silence comes
the dark ladles over
our vigilance.
We are lost now
where sleep might find us.

Where the sun greets you,
safe, with your mother
in morning's green song.

Tomato Sandwiches

How to make my husband love
the anatomy of a tomato.
He has no love for tomatoes
And still, I pack them into the cooler
with potato rolls bakery fresh that morning.

These are no ordinary tomatoes.
These are Cherokee Purple Heirloom Tomatoes.
Round as my bosom, a blossom,
color the ruby of my nipple.

It is only the two of us,
a private spot on the beach.
we soak our bones drenched in sun.
I hand him another cold beer.
Mouth of a long neck wets our lips.

He asks if there is anything to eat
in the cooler.
I offer to make a sandwich.
I begin with the meat from
the heart of an animal called summer.
I hold the plump purple-red vessel,
butcher the ripe organ of the sun.

Slice thin as paper,
stack and layer the sweet flesh
into the well of the bun.
I hand-feed him this awakening,
this new love, this small
yet undiscovered delicacy.

The Feeding of Dragonflies

The water calls,
in glossy glisten,
buoyant soft fullness,
Saying enter wash
the salty heat burden
from morning's
chore-ridden body.

The intention was there
to be productive, even in play.
To drag the thirsty kayak out,
paddle to unimagined secrets coves.

Dive in, swim like a fish,
become a loon,
drop like a stone, effortless,
dissolve fluid
only to reappear: weightless
at the other end of the lake.

Instead, I choose an air-filled cloud.
A cheap vinyl float, loudly tropical in color.
I hadn't entertained the notion of biting
flies or mosquitoes.
The only thought was to cool the body.

Dragonflies land on bare skin
on a tender cloth covered belly.
These Guardians, the only armor needed.

No better than a tub of night crawlers,
a bucket of minnows.

A shiny lure all human scented
I've become the bait of choice
for Dragonflies.

This great smallness, so expansive
in its lesson of stillness, patience,
and Presence. Here among the dragonflies.

Mercy Is a Bright Darkness

As days grow shorter,
and the hours of light become few.
The trees on their way to sleep
leave a light on before dropping their leaves.

They become torches
and lanterns, blazes of infernos,
flaming bright Pyres.

Once they have gone,
the brilliance of snow, a Shimmering brightness,
as if the moon had fallen at our feet.

See how the earth does that, saves a little light
to get us through. A nightlight for our dreams.
So we may learn to love the darkness,
as we all must do.

This taming of the dark, where roots and seeds live,
in the magic of growth and becoming,
of empathy and forgiveness.
These tender acts of nature,
reminding us
that light is everywhere, even in darkness.

The Fall

I can't believe how far the year has fallen.
How late the sunrise comes.
It was summer only yesterday.
Grateful for this small parcel of time.
This short passage that is mine.

The old abandoned root cellar
dug out near the edge of the woods.
An old log washed to the shore
notched for the cabin that once stood here.

This place that someone once built
how wondrous it must have been.
Now our own place overlooks it all.

The Blue Jays call out, cry like babies,
it's almost time for them to leave.
I will miss how they greet me each time.

Fly in low along the dirt road.
Their backs so impossibly blue
in the last of the evening light.

We have gathered the season's fallen nests,
enchanted by the mastery,
the crochet of grasses, twigs,
and bark leather.
The gifts they have held
that sing us home.

When we have long gone
Who will stand in wonder of
Our timber bones.

Duck Season

The field is full of wild geese resting,
and I want to ask them if they know
the snow is coming tonight.

I see the ducks hiding in the tall reeds.
They know it is more than snow that waits.

Come morning I will watch the sunrise,
pause and listen to the song
of ducks and wild geese winging.

And then the shatter of peace,
the sound of gunfire along the shore.

I will close my eyes to watch them,
as they make their escape.
Into the warmth of the apricot autumn sky.

The Grackle

Last summer's memory,
a hawk undressing it's prize,
a feathered oil slick,
an iridescent puddle of gasoline.
The shimmer of blues and purples,
a billow of black smoke
blowing away clean.

On a frigid spring day a grackle
hits the window. I pick it up
fume the heat of breath
into the bird's down.
It's mate shrieks wildly
from the sky, the trees,
flees and returns.

It must have seemed
I would devour the creature whole.
After, the bird, awake, alert,
blinking yellow eyes, rings of gold.

Perhaps the bird believed
It was all a dream.
As beauty sat with me
Chose the warmth of my hands,
gazed into me, studying, savoring,
this shared being alive.

How marvelous it all is,
the hawk with its hunger, mighty and golden.
The grackle in its iridescent suit of ink.

In my hand an unfolded prayer,
dresses the prize
in my fortuitous good luck.
The gift, a plume rising,
flying away free.

Black feathers harsh voice

Skeleton tree, sticks and bones

Murder in the sky

Traveling

Blue birds lined the deck rail
while blue jays watched in the pines.

Even here, where a city highway hums
near enough.
The days crowd a peopled thicket.

Alone in bed
I am offered comfort as a sandhill crane
trumpets outside the window.

Geese pass over offering what they can.
A song broken into pieces, breaking,
breaching a directional melody leading
a vocal compass.

The night remains carried into morning
on coyote, and fox voices,
as best my ear can see.

Though I am miles from home.
I am never far
from the wild that owns me.

Oh the bark on trees

thatched delicate as paper

Poems of earth's breath

The Wood Wide Web

A tree is not only one being
it is all the trees around it.
An entire forest is one living
breathing thing.

Yet trees touch sky,
a scraper, a whisk to clouds
of the blue dome above.

The canopy of trees keeps a space
between each tree and it's branches,
a respectful distance
an unspoken blind boundary.

Underneath, they are holding hands.
Roots send messages,
I am in trouble, protect yourself,
grievances they do not hold
among themselves.

Minerals mined with roots shared.
Trees leave inheritance, treasure
to the family rooted around them.
An Aspen to an Oak a Spruce,
to a Sycamore, a Hemlock to a Cedar,
a Birch or Maple.

I love you, take what I have, be well.
Live and pass it on when your time comes.
If only we were like trees. Touch sky,
not to crowd or compete,
only to share, mingle roots,
hold hands with the earth.

A Place to Store Everything

Too big to contain,
where does one find
such a containment?
And would we even want to?
When we are trying to hold
the enormity of the world.
To own such a space, a container.
I would say is often the heart,
a living memory box.
In search of a more tangible space.
I resort to a small handmade vessel,
a mending of earth gifts.
This space, though small, often holds
full gardens, the future the memory of
orchards and forests. A host to hope, to life.
This space humble yet sacred, so filled
with the magical renderings of possibilities.
This is the place to hold gathered seeds.

Inside the Seed Box

What becomes
of gathered treasure
of galvanized hope.
What rattles the seed
of a fallen tree.
The raspy voice whispers
It's promise from inside
a round box
made of bark
its own kindred vessel.
The lid laced and
stitched in white bone
of porcupine quills,
gently hemmed
In the fragrance
of sweetgrass.
To open the lid
we must first
believe
in the gather
and share
of seeds
be open
to possibilities
beyond ourselves.
Imagine the spirit
of great and ancient
trees tumbling out.
For it is something
of great reverence
to plant a tree.

The Birth of Peace after the Fire Has Gone

Oh Pandora,
gently loosen your grip,
ever so lightly lift the lid
of the box. Let fly out,
a glorious bird. In the
hope we might find
empathy within
the escape.

Loyalty

I had a dog so loyal,
He never left my heart,
weathered any storm
at my side till the end.

The trees on our street
have sheltered us
like loyal friends.
Holding back the rain,
the blistering heat
of summer.

Tonight, we can hear the sky
try to crack open.
The wind blows in,
fills my pillow like a sail.

The storm winds are strong
bowing the faith of our loyal trees.
A large branch falls into the street,

struggles in the wind,
like a giant dog still alive,
lifting its green head and legs.

A neighbor boy rushes outside,
flashlight in hand.
Does he see what I see?
The dying green dog of a loyal tree.

The Mother

The little boy, four or five
crouches the earthy
aroma, sits with the frog,
and the earthworm.
With his own blind,
amphibious roots.

Digs, stirs, mixes,
the puddle, the earth's
wet blackened gains.
The broken stick,
the coarse grass to poke.
The feather to adorn.

What life he will build
of pestle pollen mortar.
His mother beckons
him home, calls
to his hunger.

This mother...
All over his hands,
earthen and black,
brown and sandy.

She feeds much more
than his belly.
So much more,
with this pie, this cake.

Than the milk and bread
of his mother's table.

The First Osprey

Desolate cold
early spring.
Evening sun's
last blaze
A fire hawk at dusk.

The trees hadn't greened.
The lake freshly open
quickens, becomes one
fish alive.

The tables have turned.
Suddenly to become
the curious fascination
of a magnificent creature.

wild of wild,
here in
the kingdom of power.
Wildness swoops in
glides so close turns
a yellow sun eye
locked to mine.

For an instant,
I too am an
astonishment a wonder,
if only for a brief
passing moment.

In this wild
province of royalty,
I taste a privilege
outside my humanness.
In this becoming…

Returning

I don't know why I stayed away so long.
Traveling now to the end of the good road,
to where old corduroy peeks out from dirt and rock.
Where someone once tried to build a road to god.

A gathering of boulders
memories of glacial descendants.
The sound of thirst quenching
Into its own throat.

The place where eagles come
to watch their own shadows.

At night I sprawl across the dock
to watch the northern lights inform the night sky,
as owls answer back across the lake.

Come morning a loon is catching fish feeding her baby,
as it yips like a pup for more. The loon's song
haunts, echoes like a train whistle,
leaves me lonesome before I've even left.

The fork of an old two rut.
Green wild as fur dotted in daisies.
Pearls on parted emerald waves.
There, I can almost see my old dog
waiting, tail wagging,

welcoming me back to my belonging.
And I only hear I love you from the ever
present ghost of loves past.

Nine Lives

A cat is an extension of the wild,
they bring it to us bits at a time.
A tempering of power, one of
danger and surrender.

Our cat came to me when I called him in,
climbing from the lushness of the garden,
the cool undercurrent of growth, pressed
the remains of dusk and midnight
against my bare leg and ankle.

Slugs hitching a ride on the small camel of his body,
the soft pony of his fur. I pull them off the tiny wet sea lions,
their antennae a wonderment from the wilds of earth's
darkened underbelly.

He watches with green grape eyes, as the tiny creature slides
slick as a a palm reader, glides across my open hand,
creating shiny new life lines,
stretching out in pristine clear slime.

At times, that cat smelled of sunshine,
of sod and herbs, all catmint and lavender,
as he smashed against our hands and face
and we tried to breathe in his bumbling rumble.

Other times it was all mystery and wonder,
unfolding In this borrowing of time.
Holding on for the ride as many times as we could.
As if we had 9 lives.

As if we could make summer and time last forever.
All of our days are numbered,
yet he comes to me still walking the fields of snow
with only his shadow left nestling near.

Footprints in Snow

Ice fossils, soul prints
Frozen short-term memories
Paint a well-worn path

crystal foot notes
Clinging skeletal remnants
Linger unmelted

Wake forgetful sun
Come make these
watery bones
Insignificant

The First Christmas Parade since Pandemic

At the end of the parade, the sugared street,
the dung laced wake of draft horses
monumental and black,
fog pouring from the furnace
of their nostrils and bit stopped mouths.

Hallelujahs and hosannas still hung,
strung across the night air,
on a flatbed of floating magi.

Before them, fire engines, and
police fleets, throw buckets of candy,
hitting the streets like heavy precipitation.
Giddy children, gather the festivities harvest.

Gingerbread houses,
Christmas trees,
dogs in costumes.
The Grinch and Santa dancing.

Among us, tiny and newborn
pandemic babies are everywhere.
The precious, wrapped and swaddled.
These babes on this season of hope,
light the dark and the crowd.

Hunger during Pandemic

Loading the dishwasher
I realize I'm hungry.
Hungry for the overflowing of
my granddaughter's favorite tumbler,
for the too many glasses, and mounds
of coffee cups with all their mismatched
colors and logos from places that seem
lifetimes away, a Jackson Pollock painting
suspended on the top rack.

The silverware herded like dirty cattle
into their stalls, corralled with slotted
spoons and spatulas. The stacks of plates
from my sons visit. The greasy bowls
from his favorite chili.

The smell of fresh bread still in the air.
The cream clinging on the pan
from my daughter's favorite dish.
The beer mugs and stemware,
the dessert plates from
my nieces overnight stays.

The mornings full of guest dishes,
all with the hustle and bustle
rinse and clink, among voices,
conversations, and laughter.
Children and pets underfoot.

Stepping over toys
as I feed the dishwasher,

stuff it full of memories,
and messiness.

And this chaos is what I crave
what I so hunger for. As I place
My lone coffee cup,
next to my husband's empty plate…
and the cat tries to climb inside
this ravenous cavern
because,
even the dishwasher is lonely.

A Mirror to Beauty

The human world has shut down,
Yet nature is more alive
in our absence.

Today I watch maybe a thousand
diver ducks fly in.
I should be at work,
I should have missed it!

They arrive in layer
upon layer. Dip into the lake,
Landing, disappearing
into the grey of the day.

They move like fluid clouds
of spring midges
Undulating over the lake.

The silvered surface
Marred alive
with feathered beauty.

Holding Love

When spring comes
all breathy and green.
How the blooms only
last a little while.
I saw you in them.

I know this truth,
we can be made new,
and live forever.

I hear bells,
and Tibetan bowls humming,
and great tribal drumming.

I hear these without ears,
see them without eyes .
feel them in my being
though I have no body.

Love is holding the light
when all the world is dark.
Holds you without hands
without arms.

If we love the world
and ourselves too,
could it mend it all.

Will you still know me
when the metamorphosis
Is through.

When I return
to hold you
without hands
without arms.

The Lunch Date

Something so simple
as you at a desk
peeling an orange.
The share of your hand
to mine, to lips.

Sat with nothing more
than the dander and husk
of your orange peel,
after you left.

Thoughts of your fingers
unearthing the
Segmented fruit.
Taking in now, how I smell
so sweetly of citrus.

The Totem

A spirit older than the land
came to me in a dream,
as a beautiful deer.

The largest I've ever seen.
The great doe walked toward me
towering tall, as she reared up
walking only on hind legs.

Her hooves morphed
and she took my hands.
Held them with all the
gentleness of a mother's hand.

Then she spoke,
saying never stop kissing the earth
and loving the land, sky and water
for the spirit is older even than this world.

She invited me to touch near her heart.
There, I felt a wound that matched my own.
Ask yourself she said, what wounds
are greatest in your heart?
For we are mending a world
through mending ourselves.

Milkweed for Monarchs

Hear the words
brush our dreams
against what isn't there.

Asclepius, Asclepius
the genus that is your milkweed.
Named for the god of medicine and healing
The only place to fuel the metamorphosis.

There was a time we watched them
fling themselves toward the sun,
a million marigold winged flames.
And we have to wonder what if anything
we were sending them to.

Today they set like suns
over church steeples,
1,000 temples lit.
Cathedrals of forest Glenn
and prairie, farm and field.

In fall they hang like ornaments
on the cedars over Lake Michigan,
along Peninsula Point.

The migratory generation,
the last and longest lived of the year's season.
Migrating to the mountains of Mexico
resting the winter in the pine oak,
fir and mixed forest; surviving

Each year they become less.
Searching for a lifeline that isn't there
A path a link to the generations

A barometer of wings,
begging the gods.
Searching for a medicine
telling our fate.

Opera for the Moon

In the depth of nightfall darkness
narrows the distance of sound.
Where owl voices arrive to speak
 in rhythmic wooded tongues.

.

The loons are here too, they fill the room
with warbled ballads, hymns and psalms.
Though I will not find their dark bodies.

The fox and wolves will join the opera,
with peeper harmony and bullfrogs
on tenor and bass.

The silk moth thrashes its great body
against the shuttered window to applaud.
While the Luna moth sings in pheromones
from the branches.

The fireflies, those ambitious little specs
of fallen stars, lend their light.

Oh how I envy the bats in silent velvet flight
as they navigate a dark sea.

It is all a language that has so much to say
to someone or something.
As the moon speaks to everything
in pulls of light. I know it is all a door
to a darkness I can only hope to enter.

Crone Wisdom

I am that old woman,
glacial ice melting in her tea,
knowing honey is more scarce than gold.

The Bee Keepers Prayer

When I've outlived my days
in weary bones,
and the skin thins to paper.
When these eyes no longer seek the sun,
bury me in a wild field.
a meadow lined in apple trees.

Lay me out as feral
among the dandelions and clover,
and all the wild rambling things.

Remember me in the sowing of seeds.
let me feed the the flowers and trees,
then visit me in jars of honey.
and in the gardens on bees buzzing above.

Look out at all these lovely things,
I will be there in all of them
making the world go on
in bits and pieces
carried by the bees.

The Flower

No one warned her how it would be.
It started off simple enough.
She inherited the old rose bush.
And the two pots of petunias
for a housewarming gift.

How was she to know
it was contagious,
addicting even.

As she awaits daffodils and tulips
to be over run with Bearded Iris
and Lillies. From Peonies to Anemones.
The Tall Thistle, Purple Cone flower,
Bee balm, Fox glove, daisy and Aster
and of course, the rows Lined
with zinnias, and marigolds.
The earth pours out like a prism.

It happened almost by accident.
Beads of perspiration collect
under her eyes like freckles
in the hot sun, and Sweat Bees
of metallic green
sip at the nape of her neck.

She's been at it so long
she has no idea she's become
a flower.

The hummingbirds, and butterflies,
just like the bees don't bother
to scatter and leave anymore.
As she bows and bends
on her own two stems.

Delphiniums

Chosen on a whim for their color.
Tenacity to match elegance
 a magnificent surprise.

They were six feet tall and still they
try to reach for a sky they seemed to
want to be. We watched them climb
a ladder of green, before unfolding
origami in the sun, a deep color
saturation of stars in daylight.

Hummingbirds and bees sip at this celestial
open cup, and still they keep reaching unfurling
a wide indigo, lapis, and cobalt galaxy of
blossom upon endless blossom.

When the night fell silent and dark
the moths arrived in silken velveteen robes,
a kind of worship saved for the moon's eyes.
A beauty that wasn't wasted in the dark, but
known by another love.

Passing Through

Tonight the stars fell straight
from the sky like rain.
Disappearing into nothing

Light years gone without a whimper
only the fall of hearts pounding
as they fell like dimes from a pocket

Do we live enough in this world
to know each other,
when I walk in yours,
and you in mine,
and is that even enough?

So we cannot fall into nothing
disappearing into earth to air
like atmospheric drops
elements of dust and star
Making us all into dimes
already spent

A Swim in the Tannins

Young and foolish,
I believed grief was something to wear,
The earthen perfume on a mourning shawl,
a simple black dress, a dark somber suit,
or the face washed bare.

I know now it is something that takes you,
immerses you fully.
 It does not matter how many times
we enter. The solitude remains.
A nakedness tethered to your aloneness.

I suppose It is something like the river or lake
crystal, clean and clear.
You can see the bottom, the fish, the stones.

Until one day it happens,
the enormity of all that has lost its battle
or simply run its course, seeps in, steeps
into a tea. Becomes an infinite darkness,
bottomless.

The fish still very much alive,
go on living,
though you cannot see them.

There it is,
the chance to tread water,
or simply drown in the depths of grief.

And if you are lucky enough,
Swim…
in the dark loss of everything.

What I Leave You
Things to Hold and Carry

If anything I want to say,
the birds sang and I listened,
and found something to soften
the world's edges.

Hear the myriads of geese that
squeegee above our dreams,
announcing the arrival of seasons.

Mornings full of watermelon skies
all flocked in starling seeds.

And all the miraculous ordinary
in between. In all it's a fleeting wonder.

The timeless gift of love
with its invisible bonds, that forever
bind us to each other.

If anything happens,
I want to say I arrived hungry,
and dined with the eyes of my heart.
I want to say I did it with arms wide open
to love in abundance, and left a legacy of plenty.

I want to say the birds sang and I listened.
For life is a generous lover
curated for the thief
take nothing for granted.

Acknowledgments

PREVIOUSLY PUBLISHED in these fine publications:

Haiku/ OH THE BARK OF TREES/ Susan Lane Foundation/ Art Through Literature, Winner of the Heritage Haiku Contest

SPRING ON LAKE MICHIGAN/ Walloon Writers Review/ Marquette Monthly Magazine/SUPERIOR VOYAGE, Gordon Publications

DUCK SEASON/ ROOTS, Poetry Society Of Michigan Anthology

A YOOPER TAKES SHELTER AT CAMP/ Walloon Writers Review/ SUPERIOR VOYAGE, Gordon Publications

THE FALL/ SUPERIOR VOYAGE, Gordon Publications/ Marquette Monthly Magazine

BATHING BEAUTIES/ SUPERIOR VOYAGE, Gordon Publications

HUMMINGBIRD WATER/ SUPERIOR VOYAGE, Gordon Publications

UNTITLED MEMORIES/ Bangladesh Observer/International Poetry Collection

A HEARTFELT THANK YOU to my poetry family, The Marquette Poets Circle, who never fail to inspire with their kindness, generosity, and friendship. I love you all. With special thanks to Janeen and Rick Rastall, and Martin Achatz for their commendable efforts to promote poetry in everyone and the world at large. A big thanks to Carolyn Riker, Martin Achatz, and Julie Cummings for their wonderfully generous blurbs!

Printed in Great Britain
by Amazon

32268171R00061